Wrestling with the Angel

ALSO BY JENNIFER M. PHILLIPS

Sitting Safe in the Theatre of Electricity
A Song of Ascents

Wrestling with the Angel

Poems of Spiritual Exploration

JENNIFER M. PHILLIPS

RESOURCE *Publications* • Eugene, Oregon

WRESTLING WITH THE ANGEL
Poems of Spiritual Exploration

Copyright © 2024 Jennifer M. Phillips. All rights reserved. Except for brief quotations in critical publications or reviews, no part of this book may be reproduced in any manner without prior written permission from the publisher. Write: Permissions, Wipf and Stock Publishers, 199 W. 8th Ave., Suite 3, Eugene, OR 97401.

Resource Publications
An Imprint of Wipf and Stock Publishers
199 W. 8th Ave., Suite 3
Eugene, OR 97401

www.wipfandstock.com

PAPERBACK ISBN: 979-8-3852-3018-1
HARDCOVER ISBN: 979-8-3852-3019-8
EBOOK ISBN: 979-8-3852-3020-4

09/17/24

*In grateful memory of
Victor and Mavis Phillips,
my parents, who read poetry to me
from birth*

CONTENTS

You Don't Have To Be Afraid | 1
Again, From the Beginning | 2
Friends of Diogenes | 3
The Hound of Heaven, Part Two | 4
Quarry | 5
Wolf | 6
Gnosis of An Agnostic | 8
Little Brother | 9
Canteen | 10
The Mercy-Seat | 11
Light Speed | 13
Christmas Present | 14
Solar Eclipse Ritual | 15
Like Elijah, In the Year of COVID | 17
St. Seiriol's Church, Ynys Môn | 19
Leaning Over the Rails | 20
Transients | 21
Lost In Translation | 23
Elemental Energy | 25
How To Send a Condolence Message | 27
The Red Eft | 28
The Mackerel Boat | 29

Fireflies | 30

Where From and Whither? | 32

A Sort-Of Happy Holiday | 34

Resting At Sea | 36

Ely Cathedral | 37

The Oldest Place | 38

No-Prayer In a Dream of No-Place | 39

Ascent of Mount Tabor | 41

Monastiri | 43

The Dandelion Clock | 45

Annie Parson In Her Pulpit | 46

Annie Parson At Her Altar | 47

Change In the Weather | 48

Getting There | 49

Early Rising | 50

The Most Answering Things | 51

Extreme Ephemera | 52

Weathering | 54

The Other Side | 55

Madonna and Child | 57

Surprise | 58

In Need Of Body-Work | 59

Box Camera | 60

When You Can Only Proceed By Torch-light | 61

The Search | 62

Acknowledgments | 65

About the author | 67

YOU DON'T HAVE TO BE AFRAID

You can choose not to be afraid
the way grass grows from its center out
after every mowing,
in rain after long drought.
You, too, re-emerge
as from the small green fire in those close cells,
even in their lying down under the snow,
even under their dying.

Someone will always be handing you
their luggage of rage and despair,
their glasses with the lenses painted over,
their one-way ticket to doubt
if you put your hand out for it,
if you can't stand still and set it down.

So sit down at the oak table.
Let your dread take the opposite chair.
Pour the coffee. Break and share the bread and salt.
Behind the two of you, past the open window
light is going about its business
raising up the new leaves, rinsing them in its fuel of delight,
whether or not you can believe you might be saved
or anything be liable to salvage.

If you muster courage, even as much
as one small grass-blade in ten thousand
brandishing its single drop of dew
for the sun's transmutation,
it will be enough.
This is how love works.
It will bring you through.

AGAIN, FROM THE BEGINNING

I have a bone to pick with you, Almighty Architect of all this.
What did you think would happen
when you poked a hole in the emptiness
and whispered light into it — a beam
into the box of the sky's emulsion —
starting soil precipitating, imps of proteins set a-dance?
Camera, inner sight, photograph, your face
multiplied, looking back, upside down.

And they were fruitful, and craving,
and as curious as you.
Surely you were not surprised, were you,
to lose them soon to caves
where they spat out running
ochre horses and auroxes all gerund and magic,
and ate inappropriately from any tree they chose,
whispered among themselves,
while the garden where you had left them
became much too quiet. It's past time
you confessed to your initial loneliness and need,
negotiated fresh points of entry,
cheered their rowdy games, explained
your cryptic lines and processes.

Now we have the family album,
secrets coming out,
and we are mad, and packed, and leaving
home. You stand at the door
backlit. You wait. You watch us go.

FRIENDS OF DIOGENES

When it's dark again in the mornings
and nothing invites you out of yourself,
staring at the black pane,
freighted by so many losses,
until your own reflection sucks you back in,
you might as well launch out
into the dark itself, put on its skin of rain,
its wet wind breathed in, its otherness
devoid of memories, a real presence
larger than the gap between broken halves
a priest holds up,
free of postulates or domestications.
Here the self tastes its edges
and learns to turn off its tired machine;
discovers it is not abandonment to stand alone
as you do then,
sensing your heart's distance.
Night and weather wrap you in a mysterious intimacy
you might come to regard as love
once you have given up
looking for lost currency where the light is.

THE HOUND OF HEAVEN, PART TWO

Today, Great Mystery, you are the scouting dog
circling ever wider on every scent in the tangle
I plunge through clumsily and with much noise.
Silent, off to my left, off to my right,
then far ahead, or dropped back for something missing,
your eyes bright in the gloom, and always knowing
just where I am when I fancy myself alone,
with you rabbited off in the undergrowth.
I fail to see how you are braiding all our journeys,
mine and the creaturely pack you continue to claim.
You pursue us into our murky burrows and tunnels,
the graves we are quick to dig and to occupy. You
sit patient at the foot of our foolish heights
until we come down one way or another,
and wait by the window of our wild explorations
before we have the thought of coming home,
and when we, at last, sit with an arm around you
long enough to pay deep attention to your presence,
we are shocked to discover that you have rolled in our scent.

QUARRY

It's hunger, defining, new
every morning,
coloring the eye

searching hawklike
for God pouring through the grass
a small and potent fur

familiar with bleeding
and vulnerability and still
willing to be seized.

WOLF

Narvik, Norway

Almost close your eyes, the Sami shaman says,
Watch the fire. Look for *Sarahkku*, spirit of the fireplace.
In the flames, it is the wolf-*ghazzi* lifting her lips
after the hunt to sing. At the edge of the fire, I tip
my libation. *Sarahkku* guards, and eases pain
for women carrying life and laboring
to deliver it, and this is a birthing howl I bring.

Uhksahkku guards the door. She is fierce
against intruders and thieves. Call twice
outside, and wait for an invitation. In desperation,
you may enter, taking nothing away, only to warm.
She watches over the children of the house. Do them no harm.
Leabeolbmai is bow-lady. She prospers the hunt and the drum.
Use thankfully. Waste nothing. Give back. Stand firm.

Raise a *joik*, a song, a tribute, to them and whomever
blesses you. Make libation. Pour yourself out, peaceful and
    tender.
Those are the three spirits that rule the house
and strengthen the woman who keeps it, and those
she calls family. Earth-house, who is guarding your door?
When we spill the fire, who will pour
water, provide sustenance, when we squander?

I want to speak of redemption. This I believe in,
but it is lament that keeps rising through me, keen,
bitter sap. There are poets everywhere,
a hullaballoo of singing, but my share
seems like a falling drone of pipes' releasing air
after the piper's elbow lifts and the chanter
lets go of melody in the battle's clatter.

The last Tasmanian's bones were portaged, labeled, and boxed
to a British museum of lost curiosities
a grave of disinterred masks, potsherds and skeletons.
The last speaker of some local language dies
every month and a more final silence spreads.
We swim more in fraudulent chatter
than true mythologies, these days.
This is my love's stutter,
the last wolf's howl to which there comes no answer.

GNOSIS OF AN AGNOSTIC

Such a chattering of mind
like teeth in a sudden freeze! To a shivering woman
skin and teeth become everything she knows.
The whole world may flash and holler till its fade-out
but all she senses is this slap of air on bare skin.
Skin and teeth, the animal gnosis
of our, and every footed kind, what we return to.

I can square my clocks, come Spring, but for thinking of God
there's no formula. Light's lazy eights like the midnight sun
or the lurch and lapse into polar night,
fear of falling or advancing; light with
the heaving and stamping of its galey horses, too near now
in the close, dangerous dark.

When it comes to faith, agnosis is my way of keeping it.
Having mystery's back. Refusing to choose
this disloyal certainty or that one. Crossing the wires.
This is music's echo chamber, and the nautilus
I find I must enter blindfolded to hear.

We are amnesiac, we, determined to record everything;
but now, nothing is true but our forgetting
where we have been and what we may have done there.
Never again turns into everywhere always,
the way the climbing toddler topples the bookshelves over.

LITTLE BROTHER

America, my young brother
you are keeping bad company these days,
swapping bravery for bravado,
racketing night after night.
You have grown too big for your own house,
fists too eager, voice too loud.

Every morning the jays arrive
with their stormcloud-colored shoulders,
their dapper uniforms in hues of blue,
staking claim among the seed
and sending off the sparrows
with lancet beaks and eyes
until there is nothing left —
tyrants of this empire of insatiety —
taking pleasure but no joy.

My brother, when did rage become your station?
On constant guard
you stand outside yourself in its mayhem-glow
until every other is backlit as your rival,
every rival as your enemy.
Raging, you can forget you are so afraid
of everyone,
teetering on the I-beam
over your own ruined city
daring anyone to take your weapons
or your hand,
wondering how far you must walk out
to stop hearing your mother weep.

CANTEEN

Every immigrant carries a canteen of tears across the borders,
even those relieved to leave, or leaving nothing behind them
but trouble. The past's straight trunk having once forked,
we take a new shape, adopt a crabbed or a graceful stem.

More likely, both. Escaped by the skin of our teeth, or
condemned and seized by it, turned into greed's grim cargo;
arriving promise-flushed, or loss-abraded and footsore.
All of us have skin in this liminal game of come and go.

Our lives depend on welcome, whether by kin or strangers.
Welcome, we seize as entitlement, is, truly, sheer blessing,
whether we're funneled by birth into this continent of dangers
or carried by air, boat, feet, container, for our crossing.

If, once excused our debt, we refuse to forgive another's,
how will we sleep securely in our own beds
in this country we've emptied of friends, sisters, brothers,
and filled with imagined enemies instead?

THE MERCY-SEAT

Every child arrives in this world an asylum-seeker,
knowing no face, no smell of yeast rising
from skin, no voice music,
lifted into the scorching air, the lethal light,
the pulseless cold of history's blue room.

The fortunate ones soon
feel love's warm drumbeat against the cheek,
find a mouthful of grace
before they even know to stretch fingers toward it,
before the new body becomes *mine*.

Every child has traveled from one foreign country to another
like currency withdrawn from safety's pouch
to be ruled in the hand valued or valueless.

You, yourself, before you understood it
threw yourself at mercy's feet
hoping for a hearing.
You grew up to be freed to walk,
and sometimes to be carried,
clutched up with kind concern when you fell.

And like the two-, four-, ten-year-olds at our borders
you, too, will stand before the bench
while one you do not recognize as judge
waits for you to plead your own case for shelter,
though no one speaks your language in that place.

What is it about giving a cup of cold water
that perplexes you? What
about being tiny, scared and alone
that once you knew about,

is now beyond your ken?
I tell you, your own kin will no longer know you
when you plead your cause in that vetting-booth.
The only safe port-of-entry will be a door
you opened or did not open then.

LIGHT SPEED

Most Fifth Avenue murderers don't ask for permission,
announce intention, or wait for applause. Most don't boast.
More wounds are inept than malicious,
I suspect, mortal but not in the way of war —
like those we inflict when we are fleshly, gouged, and desolate
   ourselves.

You will understand because you, too, have, sometime, loved
a partner all approach and no proximity
back before you read the fine-print advice
at the foot of your IRA spreadsheets:
"investments and securities carry the risk of loss."

How hungry we are for
love that moves forward on the shoulders of time,
sound and safe as houses,
living in this place of crimsoned claws,
and jackal hours turning on one another.

It is just possible to glimpse grace slipping
between strangers, its shy light barely in sight,
but summoning, no matter all this malevolence
coming at us at the speed of dark.

CHRISTMAS PRESENT

Trees washed down to their sketch.
                                     Field mere, bare.
Minus five degrees overnight
                           and at sunrise the glass still drops
Christmas morning. Crows fluffed up
                                crouching over seed
on icy grass. The heart
                      ventures out and returns quickly,
shucking off cold at the door
                         closing out the past and its drafts,
paring down to the skin and lamplight,
                                the hunker and cinch
of this moment. Come home to converse
                                 in the vernacular of fire.

There's much more I would have liked to send
                                  in brown paper
                                  and string.
Defense, strength, truth, a file for the bars,
                             a bar for the doors
for Iranians under death-sentence,
                          gulagites, beseiged Ukrainians
in the dark, the migrants at the borders,
                              even those sparrows
jigging from one foot to the other
                            in the shriveled bush.
For now, only this hot breath on the glass
                             between us, a heart
drawn on the fogged pane of the world
                            the way a child would
                            draw it.

SOLAR ECLIPSE RITUAL

Predator is not in her self-appraisal
so the first nibble is an amazement
if not to her, to us, moon-eyed
romantics for the day, playful
as Scouts beside our pitched tent
stacked with plastic glasses, paper cups full
of boxed wine and plastic-wrapped cheeses.
An about-to-be bride, veil and all,
adjusts her polarized shades
and now her groom is invisible. It pleases
her, rather, to stare up at the first bite.
Vampire moon feels bigger than she is.
The customary dazzle curiously fades.
Some crows are restless. So are some boys at fight
age, hungry for their hormone-driven raids
and skirmishes, stuck with the crowds
of moms and dads and kiddos. A girl teases
her testy cousin by the cooler who broods
then grins. The guy with empty gun rack
on his pickup shares his beer and eases back
in a lawn chair next to the long-hair, likely blue,
with the hybrid Volvo, tips his MAGA hat to see
that strange dark corner of the sky better.
Moon has her knee on the sun's neck now.
It's enough to make us shiver. Light common as butter,
purpled somehow. Two sharp blades,
Brooks Brothers under the skin, come unbuttoned
in delight. The wedding couple exchange their vow.
Backwards perhaps: the kiss and fade to black.
But this is the party, bringing us all into a strange
communion: Moon-swallow. Sun stolen and brought back
not needing a trickster raven. The original word, inaudible,
but we can believe it has been said, and all changed

by that saying, seeing this. The roadside parking lot,
its one odds-surviving elm a tree of life, is remade a garden,
a brightening patch of innocence and pardon .

LIKE ELIJAH, IN THE YEAR OF COVID

Living hidden in the cleft of the packed city,
window on the half-light shaft
and otherwise bricked under,

you've been pondering the code of the bluescreen
for some answer,
starting gun, key episode, magnetic north for a life
in which it will make a difference
to have been good
without ever having been close.

Do you remember my friend Pearl?
The one who put on makeup in the hospital,
while planked flat on her back,
from a turquoise bag always within her reach.
Second skin, though no one came to see
in the pentimento of floor seven, unit B,
at night, when passing flocks of off-duty nurses
twittered like company fleetingly in the hallway
until the great silence was wheeled in.

I have never held a sparrow against my skin,
but I can feel in this moment
precisely its vibration in my palm
nervous and pressing forward toward flight,
bewildered at its incapability,
outraged at capture.

Some of us are brave in loneliness,
in dying, or simply in solitude.
Some intolerant of crowding,
or a bit queer and chronically unsettled.
Some bristle against fate's prickles with our own.

My dear friend, today I wonder
whether you and I are simply patient,
ready to wait if necessary for ever
hoping God will turn around and see.

ST. SEIRIOL'S CHURCH, YNYS MÔN

St. Seiriol's well — a stone-surrounded seep
planed with pale light like a quartz crystal — where I bent,
snagging someone's sodden sandwich-paper out.

Nearby the ancient dovecot, mossy with ardor, longing for wings.
Condominium hive awaiting its vanished migration,
quaint cafeteria larder for hungry monks eager for plucking.

There's an altar behind the altar — vocations private and
   public —
dusty pews and knee-knurled oak, now whispery
with regret. Visitor-voices like a rattle of kicked stones.

I kneel instead in the grass, maiden-white meristems
and green blades trodden down — water combing through
my fingers, thin as the tonsured Saint Seiriol rubbing his crown.

Reluctant to leave my own litter of prayer in the limestone
   midden,
I twist and thrust it in a vest-pocket like a shopping list
for the globe's sparse cupboard, its bruise of hidden troubles.

Too many asks were encrypted under these same oaks,
before the beetled boards of the unlit altar. Seiriol,
did you plead knee-deep in the icy bay wracked with bronze
   weed?

Did you lug sin's stones to stack here, never knowing whether you
   were freed,
but trusting the tide and the word and the turning curl of wave
   and cloud,
lifting eyes and ears to the curlew's message descending from the
   battered hills,
sharp, saving, loud.

LEANING OVER THE RAILS

Leaning over the rails as the sea churns by us,
scanning for aerosol jets, crescent fins,
slivers of black or grey backs keeping us company.
We have such a longing to lay eyes on them
the way children crave the comfort of favorite teddies
or chewed and tattered blankets
as tokens of love and the safe world's mysterious holding.
If dolphins are riding our wake like Maseratis,
if minkes are circling in an industry of herring-wrangling
that seems joyful, there must be hope for us.
Something remains intact and unbothered
in the agitated whirl of our loud passage.
If humpbacks still sing over the roar of oil
and cylinders and sparks, then surely we
have some small share remaining of innocence.
We seek the glimpse, a shadow, a secret bulk
gracing us for a few moments
in its own unfathomable curiosity, an untranslatable eye.
A paddle of tail we've come to recognize
popping up like those lollipops
our guides carry to call us to our own groups,
announcing - just for now - *you are numbered one of us*.
We laugh, we point, we jog across the deck to follow
someone else's finger held out straight
like a warning angel shouting: There! There!

TRANSIENTS

The body we wake in
isn't the same body in which we slumped into sleep.
                                        Shot from time's
                                            crossbow
we are always moving
             faster than light
                         through the evolving air,
every routine, a fiction.
This new moment slaps us into being.

The same old pine by the window
                           immortally tall
is pushing its new pith out into cork
                         cell by cell,
                                pinching and popping
into a fresh constellation.
                    Its resin-scent on the tepid air
is a blind-man's-bluff of frantic molecules
I snuffle in as I click the car's lock open.
Years of minute oxidation
                    for the first time, today
                          make the hinges
                          squawk.

There are no do-overs in this life.
                        Between foundation wall crack and
                        burdock stem
a mouse scoots on its last journey
                        under the gyre of the sharp-
                        shinned hawk.
Here we are
in the one precious instant between now and then,

like sparks struck from steel and stone. What can we do?
Be tinder. Become fire.

LOST IN TRANSLATION

Wind from the Northeast, coming this way,
but its hands are empty
                      and it's not talking.

The shadblow bushes are all a-shiver with finches,
Fusillades of song,
                      the content lost in translation.
In my own backyard,
                      I am at sea. Inscrutability
on all sides. Squirrels, birds, foxes,
even the trees are all talking to each other. Not to me.
                                            Keeping
                                            secrets.

I have a well-rehearsed commitment to contentment
that settles the mind like a benign occupying force,
                                    while rations
                                    last.
Still, I can't help but notice —
everything is keeping its secrets close to its chest.
                                    What could we
                                    expect
who long since shattered our contract with this world?

                                    Do you also
practice contentment like a life-jacket drill
on shipboard in rough weather?
                            Do you scan the local scene
for its signals sent,
                      Then bend to listen for its content meant?
What is it saying to you — the lost world
                                  you try to describe daily
                                into being

and hope for —
for and in and to yourself?

ELEMENTAL ENERGY

Do you often wonder whether
you are out of your element,
buzzing round importantly and yet

like a stray electron
without reins or bonds
or a place that is your own?

And do you wonder,
does this make you dangerous, rogue
in the curious world of people

daring to approach?
In an old study, public librarians
were assigned to brush — or not — a hand

of every visitor being handed back their books
and then at the door,
asked by another, how is your day?

Those touched
said they were happier, having a better day.
Likely, too, went out

inclined to hear wren-songs
through the traffic din
and notice the confident sideways-look

of the child looking up at the dad
holding his hand, standing
at the crosswalk. Signs of love everywhere.

Know this: your element is weightless,
exciting as car window air blast
when you were six, sticking your head out.

Here and now, your charge
is just the thing all those strangers
don't yet know that they are hungry for.

HOW TO SEND A CONDOLENCE MESSAGE

I also woke to the magnanimity of this morning,
expectation a basket of oranges on my kitchen table,
yet agnostic as any of us cracking this day on the edge of the frying pan.

My back steps need a dollop of paint. Dust squares up under the bookcase.
Somewhere in me settles the pool of tender-enough language
to finger my old friend's fresh loss across distance with love's *Yes*.

The rest can wait. The sharp-shinned hawk took another dove yesterday
in my garden, fluffs of indecent under-down will stay snagged in the grass
longer than I think I can stand, while the other birds keep their custom,

coming and going, a lone dove now among them. I refill the millet,
clumsy before their mystery. What else can we offer from sympathy's
separate paltry stores? Silence only helps from beside, so we find words.

THE RED EFT

Away from family for the first time, must have been summer after
   fifth grade
at camp in the Adirondacks, hiking up a logging road
in an ancient forest of hemlocks, craggy roots vivid with moss,
and a few long-since felled trunks dissolving into soil
black with is wealth of death and life, laced with white mycelia,
bustling with woodlice and small black beetles.
I jogged at the back of the horde of boisterous campers,
when I heard its presence, scarlet as a shout, turning me aside.
Viridescans, its name defines it,
delicate as glass but seeming soft
and blurred, having no edges, like flame,
making its two-year spirit-ramble between pond and pond
where it will drab again amongst the weeds, go down to gills.
Finding me, the child dangerous as a moving mountain,
larger, surely, than a newt can make sense of —
we of the loud and heedless feet thumping through the branches.
You turned me aside from that mob of girls
who went on, bickering and laughing up the trail
bug-slapping in denim and madras.
You sang to me and I
have never been the same.
You were so still, as though you had not finished
materializing in this world you were passing through,
and if you had a word to speak to me from the damp bark
it would be *Look!* it would be *See!* —
but don't touch. *I have not yet arrived where I am going,
and neither, girl, have you.*

THE MACKEREL BOAT

If you had stood at this same dockside sixty years back
you might have spotted Elmer Davis,
who didn't care much for children,
stowing the rods, the gaff, the buckets,
chomped on his cold pipe,
flannels cuffed to the elbows,
taking a gamble on the wee watchful girl
because she never chattered or fidgeted
or like himself said much at all,
sat quiet as an old pine between the granites
watching the wake unspool.
Look for the patch of bubbles,
the minute motion from below amid the huge motion,
the tiny blown foam different
from all the blown salivation of the ocean
where mackerel and pollack school following the pogies.
And she did.
Showed her how to bait and throw
the line out athwart with only a word or two and a flick.
Her wrist picked it up as quickly as the slivers of silver rose and
    bit.
He noticed how she watched the mottled muscley heave
twitching heaped in the pails.
How it hooked his innards that she sat
hunched and uncomplaining in the cold and wet
watching with a shocked wonder
the light go out of the bright scales.

FIREFLIES

Waiting for the Perseids,
the odd trickle of light
between domestic constellations,
we're knee-high in field-grass, around us
the sky tucked in at all its edges.

There's such expectation —
like being six again on the way to the pony corral
for a magical circle or two on a mythic back —
anticipating our yearly intersection with the dust
of this cosmic arena that we and it keep passing through.

And there is one! Drizzling down the East,
evaporated quicker than wishes.
Cassiopeia has no time to turn on her throne.
And another! Dripped and fizzled
through the bottom of the holey dipper.

What an affinity we have for particles finding their ending here,
like tiny Vikings blazing out in their sea of night.
Half an hour — nothing — *a dud,* you say, disappointed.
   Are those clouds coming?
A short show of it!

Sweet alfalfa must lifts on the breeze.
Sough and lash of grasses tickling our shins.
And then begins the August girandole
and glitter of fireflies, not falling but rising,
in their thousands, seeking each other, the great desire

leaking in on our every side
as though through pinpricks from a brighter room.
Our universe a dark lantern signaling.

We, too, prickles of light among signaling stars, and fireflies —
brighter and more lasting than we realize;
and yes, even the dust.

WHERE FROM AND WHITHER?

It's everything we want
to ask a stranger passing
when we ourselves are lost

and passing, but cannot
ask where we are together.
Are we merely taking notes to be totted

at last in catalogs of dismissal?
Found in countries we unmap?
Described in lines we redraw then scumble?

So, tell me one true thing
from your scuffed heart,
from its healed seam.

Lay your fingers on
my wrist while you relate
your myth of origins

snugged smooth as sheets,
all you have brought
to point to, to point out

like Verrazzano, leaning hip to the rail,
naming unmet landmarks: the cape
of avarice, point speculation.

This is the blistered road
of pilgrims. Only the mazed
walk here humbly enough,

not knowing the way,
while the old land hums
under our soles

its holy music.
Lost, maybe we too become holy,
people of nothing but silt and humus,

a bit more spindrift in history
whited-out around us
in a pass of mountained snow.

Keep calling out, stranger.
I need your voice
to be nearby.

I'm sure I will never be wholly
known to myself
without you.

A SORT-OF HAPPY HOLIDAY

Opening a fifth in place of presents
to an old movie from an era of snow and repentance
and fedoraed men with turned up collars heading home,

lamps always lit among the bookcases,
and star-eyed scrubbed kids in poinsettiaed dresses.
This is not then. All the places

you might walk upstairs to, stay awhile
and pay for at a battered desk, are not your own.
But Mary at the market, with a sort-of-smile

slid a pair of day-old muffins into your sack,
muttered *Happy Holidays!* and your codger-twin
held the door for you into the sleet and hack

of barking traffic balking at lights in haste
to get wherever they wanted most to be,
while you doddered off at a more patient pace.

The Holy Family in a plaster huddle,
wind-chipped, decorates the local square,
bedraggled without benefit of stable.

You say you are grateful for a roof and a door that locks,
and a kind look across a checkout counter.
These days, mercy-crumbs are all it takes

to get through, and none of them comes with wrap
or ribbons. It's free night, New Year's Eve on the subway
and a seat spare near the door. A wisp of scent maps

a route to memory. Even if it was
a hard-handed loud family to come up in, it was yours,
and she smelled of Toni Home Perm, and he of chaws

of Tiger Chew, and meatloaf waited most Mondays
on a set table, and everyone seemed to be scraping a way
up to a known destination, not sliding slantwise

toward avalanche, or flying a holding-pattern
waiting to spiral down. Still, there are ferns
of fractal frost ornamenting your window, a smatter

of reflected red and green in the ice,
and the radiator's cranking out its old hymn of comfort,
so, for today, the journey feels worth the price.

RESTING AT SEA

The gardener takes comfort
in the thought of someday
wedding humus and mushrooms,
resurrecting heirlooms.
I'm breeding the perfect peony,
not seeing how we are potbound in the world,
under piggybacking cumulonimbus
billowing through the thin blue air,
how fevers of lightning keep breaking out.

When silence dawdles in my ears
when bones ache, and morning
forgets to raise its shutters
I float on my dark sea, resting,
staring up at stars in a strange hemisphere.

Spare me metaphors of rescue.
God is not a helicopter, rowboat, or a rope
and I am not reaching for flotsam to cling to,
not spying out lights on any harboring horizon
while sending out S.O.S.'s,
not even aiming my small myopic glass.

It is enough, tonight, to ride this plasma in the dark,
this sea that has carried me always in its cells,
waiting for the current called hope whose pull I know.

ELY CATHEDRAL

At last, we spot the truncated cathedral
crouching Atlas-like on its puny rise
shouldering the weight of the invisible.
It soars yet is pressed down, denting the peat,
seeming to sink and lean, or as though pulled down
by our small insistent, hungry hand of longing.
Under its complicated starry ribcage
a red blaze pulses, striping its storied glory
through the doubt-congested shadows.
Coming night in the nave lays down tawny bands.
We quake as though for the tiger's stalking pads
across the cold flagstones lidding memory.
The endless dark snuffs out prayers' tiny lights,
yet, still, their whisper keeps rising and is met.

THE OLDEST PLACE

Iona

You have traveled so far to find this peppercorn of ground
along the herring-road,
in an eggshell coracle of intention,
washed of soil and all certainty,
until you have turned silver yourself.
So stand firm
where small green stones are the tears of ancient saints
on this island adamant as carborundum,
everlasting under your marsh-soaked shoes.
Granites here relax their hold
crumbling with a soft blush into this new eon.
To walk this short beach is to find yourself —
to find yourself both plaintive and glad
among the gulls and tussocks,
the bog-cotton and the ironstone sea.
Sooner than you think it will slide
back under the waves from which it rose,
like Atlantis, its name the only trace.
But kneeling now in the round of the ruined cláchan
the scent of what is holy still rises
out of the turf to encompass you.
The dovey sky with its scurf of cloud
enfolds you, mothering and still
and that in you which was so long underwater
starts to rise.

NO-PRAYER IN A DREAM OF NO-PLACE

We were standing in the rubble, Ruth and I.
She who could make prayer out of anything,

she who believes you can make prayer out of what is left
even when nothing is left,

and I with nothing prayer might be made of, standing
in the bankrupt dusk that would never be silent again,

on pulverized concrete, splinters of the impermeable
daggering the dust. We two stood in the ruins

as smoke rose, as explosion bloomed like a rose
opening too quickly, robbed of its color. *Why?* she asked.

Why are we here? I said,
Where else would God be more likely to come?

A young man long-gone from the world
with a broken-spined hymnal stumbled out of the cloud.

He pushed the book into my hands. He said,
Show me the words. I've forgotten the words.

And then I, or someone, was singing: a thin,
sweet tune, threading up lost like smoke, or like a flame.

Deck thyself, my soul, with gladness — incongruous,
that hymn of aftermath. What, ever again, could be glad?

And where the few, great, millennial blocks
still lay married on top of one another

Ruth and I bent to tuck our scribbled tatters
into those chinks.

ASCENT OF MOUNT TABOR

Not near anywhere
pimple of a mountain anywhere else a hill,
a cinder-cone, dawdling in its dormancy.

Two taxis ferry the Americans off the bus
to Transfiguration's summit,
chiseled-out road like a litter of bobbie pins to haul us up.

The Bedouin driver has no English
and we, almost no Hebrew or Arabic. Tooth-gapped grin
and driving too fast, at every switch

we grab for something and squeal
over the sheer drop as he bellows
Halleluia! Hang glide!

Flat gravel summit, iron fencing asleep on the job
warding the holy place or keeping idlers
from trampling the overgrown rose garden

where the bees bump about like drunks
and the midday smells not of rose but pine,
from below, a scent not lifting but taking us deep.

Beyond, with no sense of irony, the Franciscan church
like three bleached beer-tuns tumbled side by side,
three chapels: one for Jesus, one for Moses, one for Elijah.

It was Peter's idea. Perhaps the others slept
as they were wont to do in gardens,
missing the great befogged speaking, the prohibition,

and later wishing they had held on to him.
The gang marched in, excited. Me, I don't swallow
ambiguity. I just sit and chew and chew

on a bench, near roses in a beetled ruin
sweetly carmine, being changed
as we are, the nectar and fallen petals, bitter fruit.

Parched brightness, no trace of mist and only wind-speech
over the beautiful, irrigated plain
that close-up is mulched everywhere in plastic,

desert transformed to vegetable-basket,
tourists dunking in the muddy Johannine Jordan-stew,
fertilizer run-off greening all the pools.

Speak to me! The bees fizzed
and the pines murmured under their breath
but there was not a cloud or voice

so we squinted at each other, with fists of postcards
and olivewood trinkets,
and the sun too bright to see.

MONASTIRI

In the abandoned monastery
most prayer happened without my knowledge

as under the fig two yellow finches
pricked the grit for invisible seed

in the barren garden where thistles
poked through the cistern wall.

The few cells were dank,
a scabby concrete, doorless

as mouths of the dead. But the chapel was swept,
fallen plaster fragments heaped outside,

a candle stub melted on the stone shelf.
There I tried my best but could not speak

to the twin painted saints, Cosmos and Damian,
faded into their inwardness of prayer.

So I wandered the ruined balcony,
dangled my speculations over the low wall,

breathed the musty incense of the pines
mounding the valley like junked upholstery,

grateful for dabs of scarlet grace on the pomegranate bushes
and in the softening sky,

piled some pebbles, wondered if God would pass by
or drop in, if I were to stay the night

or carry a can of olive oil up the slope
for the empty lamps, but finally

I just walked down to supper, dusk a cool
vestment on my sunburned shoulders,
listening for the word the sea was speaking.

THE DANDELION CLOCK

The soul is in the body
as light is in the air, Plotinus thought.
Light being God's factotum —
Light, and air,
and time, so restless these three, setting off
soft detonations
of the dandelion clocks,
the thistle globes.

Every flight is risky,
is a crossing over,
a controlled fall,
hoping to set seed.
Seeing this,
no wonder we bristle and rush as we do.
Small wonder we deny so much.

Time is forever managing our damage
into finitudes, sending
all our briefs and declamations
rattling down the stairwell,
setting loose our tiny freights of hope to rise.
In time, though not quite yet
we may become
transparent with the joy of this,
even allow ourselves to be
carried over,
lifting off.

ANNIE PARSON IN HER PULPIT

She finds the weekly preaching something between
a dance of veils and a brave striptease,
each telling an unclothing of sorts

a scarf of memory shed, her heart's dropped glove,
the unpeeled stocking of longing,
the lacy underthings of her hope

and the firm flesh of Scripture,
with the clear eyes of learning, always both
looking back and outwards, speaking to the hearts.

A preacher must be shameless and alluring
but always proper - a go-between sent
to woo by proxy, love to cement the deal

for God's intentions. Annie slides the gold
bangles of a marriage-gift on others' arms,
shows off the portrait under road-dusty glass,

pours libations of blessed water and oil and wine,
offers the Name's promise, and when it's done,
goes solitary to her tea and slippers.

ANNIE PARSON AT HER ALTAR

At her altar, it seemed the bread would not break
though the words came fluent as blood,
and she could no longer read their eyes.

Hardly a touch, but nonetheless a touch
of hands. The woman whose fingers
clamp briefly like scissors her own

though kindly meant.
Those crabbed hands held sideways to hers
expecting bread to land in in defiance of gravity.

The banker who holds one hand out only
as if to shake, or - casual and grudging -
to take and run. The child, hands over head, feeling for sheer

delight. All these hands she fills, not fathoming
their deep intentions, seeing them held out
week after week, hungry for a plain loaf

rising. She takes, and breaks, and blesses,
in a movement tidal beyond sentiment,
feeling the wounds of oil and her people always in her palms.

CHANGE IN THE WEATHER

Itinerant light, November,
first here, then there.
Wind shaking its wet pelt at the door
waiting for me to go out,
every old bone conversing with the weather.

Gloom-time, I'd like to be a collector of the light
from all its nooks and crevices,
but it keeps slipping through my knuckles, like joy,
like the loose end disappearing through a knot.
The wind keeps leaning in, as though in affinity,
parsimonious sentiment in this season of abscission.

But an hour later, sunlight bustles in to dab salve on every wound.
What could have been so troubling,
so adverse when I started out? Forgotten.
On the hill's flank little bluestem waves its soft tufts
where any of us would be welcome to bed down like a deer
on the curve of the bright world
to pillow our head on its shoulder.
So, lie back with me. It is breathing under us.
Rest and let it turn.

GETTING THERE

I never imagined going into the light,
as they tell you that you should do, free of shadow
and the need for sunglasses.
God surely must be more
like a green glade, like the scent of wet moss
where the stream exhales
going about its own calm business
having spread out its welcome, saying, Rest
as long as you like,
while I go on seeing to things.
Here is a cold drink.
When you are ready, you can tell me
everything,
when the moon gets home
and after my trees have sung your song.
No, I don't need help just now.
The world is dusted
and all its sheets are clean.
Smell the mown grass like Eden
where we once lived — do you remember?
Take the easy chair.

EARLY RISING

This is the season of rising in the dark
while night condenses on the window glass,
more darkness gathered than the air can hold.
But sometimes there comes a soft sweet whispering
just before rousing from my winter night,
as when the limbs of lovers wake to discover
their entanglement, not seeking separation,
when voices of adoring and adored
are for a moment indistinguishable.
My own breath comes and goes in a larger breathing
Though solitary, I am not alone,
caught up in the arms of companionable weather
the germinating rain, the warming wind
that murmured across that vast original deep
those mysteries the Unsleeping speaks to sleep
that all will be well under the lull of it;
that just behind the darkness is the light.

THE MOST ANSWERING THINGS

These are the lively oracles of God
received in Barnstable, Massachusetts, in early June,
where bushes blur into a green wash.
Grass gilds and lolls, languorous with seed.
Everywhere — nest-chatter, secret building,
industry of early summer, gossiping close to the ground.

The local widows stroll in the afternoons,
stiff steps, soft syncopated tapping of canes
down the sea road daily to inspect the marshes.
Much has been lost. Something has been found
in the solidarity of this sliding world,
time's remainder in now more limited means.

We fill our bird-feeders, make small reparations
for the land-grab of human life since its beginnings.
We can still overhear the vanished sawn-down trees
that sough and sigh in our dreams. Our summer days
are roisterous with weed-whacking and mowers,
trucks piled with all we prevent from setting seeds.

We drift through lush Springs and the bee-drunk blush of roses
toward the spartan season yet to come.
We care for one another as we're able.
Desire focused by blessings of attenuation,
we see and hear rapaciously what is left us,
more thankful than afraid. We who will soon
leave everything, leave nothing on the table.

EXTREME EPHEMERA

For an instant I thought we could save everything
forever. Stacking the pixels tighter than particles in an atom.

Foolish notion. The 0s and 1s drizzle
out of the ethers, cables snap and go blind.

The troves bulge and slump with a weight of memory
past retrieval, the films slide by us sprocketless and hazy,

time swallows the *next* as it will the rest. I put more trust
in paper - or rag cotton - first and second anniversary stuff

when it comes to marriage, paired ink and fiber, pressed
and bound. Hands can hold its finitude, more like dimensions of
   a house

of findable corners than an infinite horizon
through which sun scrolls as though its rote were innovation.

I'm trying not to recollect the burned libraries, blurring floods
and beetled archives, picking the letters from fused parchment

like fit seeds from a withered handful - Nebuchadnezzar's
shopping list, at the end of our X-ray tomographic labors.

We are painted walls at right angles to one another, hieroglyphs
searched out and resurrected for a spell, through dust's gaps.

Time's detritus heaps up over us again. We must sharpen our
   teeth
on truth, cherishing the ephemera, the listening, the seeing.

Don't we long to be saved, to have our dream-catalog
testify: this was a person noted, able to be known by manuscript,

even, hand? Here is an invitation to parse her double meanings,
to come close. I want to be held warm in the palm

like cuneiform, a silent tablet of deep speaking still
coming to you from under the earth, from the heart's cave.

WEATHERING

Collicky weather, snorts of snow, and squalls of sleet,
wind-gouts rattling the oaks; still, I go out
for a sip of the clean impersonal air. I'll be wet

through in minutes, a way of being one
with what is, and what cannot be moved
by my misery or confusing circumstance. Come

with me, beyond concerns of comfort.
Be washed, be slapped and snapped about
by the wind, ageless, original, where our hurt

counts for nothing, yet seems to find echo,
even empathy and solace — like a cried-out child —
rest. The unmoved mover moves us to go

forward. Even the planet beneath us tips us
into the next moments of falling and rising.
Surprising — how the two are one. we will not be lost in loss.

THE OTHER SIDE

On the other side of this life,
I suspect, a trapdoor opens up
and we see where the ductwork and cables run
that keep the lights on in this world,
>   its heat, its juice.

Some of us make a late start, but we get there in the end,
for what it's worth.
Work not what we planned
or on any anticipated schedule,
but it plows the row, it feed the chickens,
>   it builds the house,
and looks a lot like love, if we are lucky.

Phone call today from Timothy down on the Blue Ridge
celebrating outdoor church in a trailer-park
under the cottonwood corbels,
saints hanging out of their aluminum sashes, praying along,
fiddler pinning his music to the hood of the Dodge with a stone.
In the world of ten thousand consolations,
crickets saw away at their gospel in the spent grass,
and a blue heron, still as immortality, stands guard at a bend in
   the creek,
>   as he does daily.
Kids crawfishing out on the stones mid-channel
stoop to reach through their reflections
to pull wrigglers up from the muck,
and I'm chewing on a stalk of little bluestem watching the water
   change its mind.
Time and tide, they say, wait for no one,
>   flooding in, then running
>   out.

How much is enough, or what is lacking? What will last?
We're always asking ourselves, whether we know it or not.

Not a sigh for the blessing of rest
                                       in the sweet by and by
Refrain from the burying ground, reaching for me.
Scent of wild grapes going by where they dangle from hedges
    along the road,
Red-tail aiming her little jets of sound and letting fly.
Another day to lean back in the arms of.
After all, this ground sustains us
until it closes over our heads,
and then still does.

MADONNA AND CHILD

They gaze down: the acanthus-crowned mother,
the weanling she is lifting to her chest
as though away to safety from some risk,
a hand on his belly, thumb braced against a rib.
Is she saying, "You will go there, but not yet,
to that bitter, thorny place turning below"?

Lids heavy, the child's inspection echoes hers,
resignation in the set of a placid jaw
but not enough, perhaps, to fend off sleep.
From one side, it seems they are smiling at the sight,
or perhaps sidelong at one another. From the other,
the sculptor seems to hint at solemn sorrow.

She is treading the moon down under slippered feet,
gazing through distance across the small room of space.
It's cosmic business they face, but also tender
and intimate, like watching with your own
held toddler a small, furred, newborn creature,
wondrous but in blind need of forbearance.

Then you see the globe already in his hands
held away from his mother, balanced on a knee,
his own familiar and secure possession,
as if from heaven, a fresh journey is about to open
with a new need, and the child has begun again.

SURPRISE

What love we make
we find made for us,
gracious. Easy to mistake

found for fashioned,
thinking ourselves the wiser,
miserly with wonder. Impassioned

under our surfaces
love sings in us all the while
like a smitten bell

stroked cochlea
a shell ringing, a cockle
full of sun and sea.

We hear, but fail to see,
wile-snared and wary
by habit, the prising gift,

love's genius lifting the lid
off our flats, letting the imp fly free
to play in found hidden joy,

wading in the blessed surprise.

IN NEED OF BODY-WORK

There's no scratch-cover polish for the soul.
Trouble scores deep. What we have chosen, we carry
past forgiveness's checkout, not skilled
at receiving what we are given,
not gracious ourselves at letting go.

I met a man long ago at a state hospital,
confessed the same teen drunken traffic homicide
he had been confessing to me and every chaplain for fifty years,
sopped brain still gripping that wheel,
knee-deep in mercy's river, dry as bone.

Move past marsh willows, hazels and sallows,
mud-gorged banks to the winding-green.
Same river they say you can't step in twice.
If I believe in today's pearl-grey cirrostratus,
brothel-purple loosestrife, and the paddling loon,

I must believe also in the river, the ocean, and the rain,
seed to new pod, water sheeting the floodplain,
sweeping clear, and the gift of starting again
in the same muddy field. Sweat. Surrender.
Scraped, soaked, and dented but freer than I know.

BOX CAMERA

What you never could believe in,
what you judge less disappointing to disparage than explore,
isn't finished with you yet.
"I just can't see a need for it!" you say, and this is true.

My first camera was a Kodak Brownie Box.
Aptly named, a box, empty of nearly everything
except its small mysteries capable of capturing
the seen world into thrall in two-tone gloss,

and still I have the skewed surprised cow
at the Catskill Game Farm staring back at the child,
the street-lamp taller than Big Ben, leaning like Pisa across the frame,
my Nana's one visit to America, her flowered Viyella dress and glass beads.

Never did quite grasp how the light outside
became the light inside,
merging with memory close enough to forever through an instant's aperture,
when really, opened up, there was nothing there to see.

A mystery. What, all my life, has been chased and chasing me
in an invisible whirl of desire, love, doubt and certainty,
glimpsed in the blur of a moment long ago,
never to be set down, never left, never fully seen. . .

now I find myself on the inside of, peering out,
and so, not seeing
that containment through which light passes
even when it is looking out through these eyes.

WHEN YOU CAN ONLY PROCEED
BY TORCH-LIGHT

Any fallen evening when the weight
of the bleak world, like wet wool around your shoulders
offers no comfort,

in the very stoop under that weight
pressing your eyes down to the sidewalk's shoulders
where the curb holds back storm-runoff like a fort

by a brown and kelpy tide, stand still and wait.
See, a low light starts caressing the shoulders
of a plantain's leaves in a stone-crack, and there is comfort,

a teaspoonful at a time, a counterweight
of grace, like a dandelion's gold that shoulders
the grass up. See it as scruff, or by blind luck or effort,

see it new as ruthless glory, throwing its weight
around the humdrum, lifting off your shoulders
despair's dark, handing you the flashlight of comfort.

THE SEARCH

What I have been seeking so long, lifelong, and so could not
   come to rest
before finding, excites and exhausts, and entices me. I could not
   come to rest!

Carried over oceans and through countries vast and message-
   laden, spread
treasure-map of traces, footprints, fresh signs, how could I stop
   anywhere to rest?

I've been pointing to you leading me on and forward: *There*, I say,
   look there!
But you have vanished, gone ahead. I sit to catch my breath like
   all the rest.

Obscure subject of desire, Scheherazade, you spin your story out,
in every rustle of grass, thistle, throstle, bloom on the drooping
   branch at rest

I know you more, and know I know you less. Yearning's its own
   revelation,
sinuous delight. I am the Eve to your apple, hungry for all the
   rest.

Weaver of wisdom, whisper your words again; but it is your fra-
   grance brings me back
to sit in your cloistered shade, among vesper roses — this garden
   of perfect rest.

A gate closes behind me. Voices drift down the path. I overhear
   argument.
Sweet moments sour. Contention erupts into wrath — another
   country of unrest!

You've made us gardeners. Soon we must settle the trammeled
   soil, rake debris,
repair our disorder, rebuild the toppled walls, labor, if we are to
   come to rest.

Then I'm on the prowl again for you. Where have you gone, first,
   best love?
Knitter of souls, I'm your dropped ball of yarn. Reach down here
   where I've come to rest.

My heart is restless. Across hobbled miles Jenifer's mind now defies physics' laws.
Grown old, I'll run to you lightly: body in motion tending always
   to come to Rest.

ACKNOWLEDGMENTS

I am grateful for their encouragement to the editors of the publications in which these poems were first published:

"You Don't Have To Be Afraid", in *Atticus Review*, 2023

"Again, From the Beginning", in *The Adelaide Literary Magazine* #66, 2024

"Friends Of Diogenes", in *RavensPerch*, 2024

"Little Brother", in *America*, 2023

"Canteen", in *The Adelaide Literary Magazine*, 2024

"Light Speed", in *The Galway Review*, 2024

"Christmas Present", in *Blue Unicorn*, 2023

"Like Elijah In the Year Of COVID", in *Ocotillo Review*, Kallisto Gaia Press, 2023

"Leaning Over the Rails", in *The Write Launch Winter Anthology*, 2024

"Lost In Translation", in *The RavensPerch*, 2022

"Elemental Energy", in *The Galway Review*, 2024

"Fireflies", in *Concho River Review*, 2023, and nominated for a 2024 Pushcart Poetry Prize

"Where From and Whither?", in *LitBreak Magazine*, 2024

"A Sort-Of Happy Holiday", in *Cider Press Review*, 2024

"Ely Cathedral", in *Dappled Things*, 2024

"No-Prayer In a Dream Of No-Place", in *The Penwood Review*, 2024

Acknowledgments

"The Dandelion Clock", in *Artemesia Anthology*, 2023

"Getting There", in *Coming Home Anthology*, 2024

"Weathering", in *Fine Lines*, 2024

"When You Can Only Proceed By Torchlight", in *Rushing Through the Dark Anthology*, Choeofpleirn Press, 2023

ABOUT THE AUTHOR

JENNIFER M. PHILLIPS is a bi-national poet, retired Episcopal Priest and AIDS Chaplain, gardener, grower of Bonsai, painter, and has been writing and publishing poetry and prose since age seven. Born in Kent, England, Phillips grew up in upstate New York and has lived in four counties in Britain, five U.S. states, and now, with gratitude, in Wampanoag ancestral land in Cape Cod, Massachusetts. Not surprisingly, her work finds recurring themes of boundary-crossing, journey, displacement and belonging. Phillips' poetry has won several awards, has been twice nominated for a Pushcart Poetry Prize, has appeared in over a hundred journals and two chapbooks: *Sitting Safe in the Theatre of Electricity* (iblurb.com, 2020) and *A Song of Ascents* (Orchard Street Press 2022). Her third chapbook, *Sailing to the Edges* is forthcoming in 2025 from Finishing Line Press. She has also authored two books of prayers: *Prayers For Penitents* and *Simple Prayers For Complicated Lives* (Church Publishing, 2002 and 2006), and several books on liturgical practice. Phillips believes a poem is like a little brass pan to carry fire's coals through the winter to others in need of warming.

www.ingramcontent.com/pod-product-compliance
Lightning Source LLC
Chambersburg PA
CBHW060423050426
42449CB00009B/2100